From

The Women's Press Ltd
34 Great Sutton Street, London EC1V 0DX

The Translators

Grazyna Baran was born in Bradford of Polish parents. She is bilingual. She studied physics at the University of Kent, and is now head of science in a London comprehensive school. She is actively concerned with issues of women and science, is married and has two children.

Margaret Marshment taught literature at the Jagiellonian University, Kraków, from 1979 to 1982, where she encountered Anna Swir's poetry and met the poet herself. She had previously taught literature at universities in Kenya and Nigeria, and she is currently surviving on a combination of teaching feminist studies and cultural studies, reviewing, writing and poetry. She has published articles on ideology in literature, and is now co-editing a book on *Women in Popular Culture*. She is unmarried and has a seven-year-old daughter.

The Illustrator

Jola Scicińska is a London-born Polish woman who works with the traditional Polish peasant art of paper-cutting. She combines traditional patterns with images from her own life, sometimes mixing paper-cut and collage. The underlying theme of all her work is 'a celebration of ourselves and our surroundings – whoever we are – as one of the necessary steps to end all oppression'.

About the Raving Beauties

The Raving Beauties are a three-woman team of actress-singers: Anna Carteret, Sue Jones-Davies and Fanny Viner. They devote a great deal of their time and energy to performing and promoting poetry by women.

Their first poetry anthology, *In the Pink* (The Women's Press, 1983), based on their prizewinning Channel 4 television show, was a best-seller; and their second, *No Holds Barred*, a collection of unpublished poems selected from some 15,000 submitted to them, was reprinted within weeks of publication (The Women's Press, 1985).

Anna Carteret has spent most of her life working in the theatre, particularly at the National Theatre, where she played leading parts between 1967 and 1982. She has appeared regularly in television plays, and as the police inspector in the BBC television series *Juliet Bravo*, but returned to the theatre in 1986 to play Mrs Sullen in *The Beaux' Stratagem* at the Lyric, Hammersmith.

Fanny Viner has achieved nothing remarkable, and is privileged to say so in print.

Sue Jones-Davies is an actress and a singer. Her most recent work includes a one-woman show called *Two-Track Mind* and a film for Welsh television called *Ysbyd y Nos*.

ANNA SWIR

Fat Like the Sun

Translated by Margaret Marshment
and Grazyna Baran

Preface by the Raving Beauties

Illustrated by Jola Scicińska

 The Women's Press

First published by The Women's Press Ltd 1986
A member of the Namara Group
34 Great Sutton Street, London EC1V 0DX

Translations of 'She Can't Sleep', 'He Treats Them to Ice-cream',
'Peasant Woman', 'Family Life', 'Two Old Women', 'The Reaper',
'Her Greatest Love' previously appeared in *Making for the Open*, ed.
Carol Rumens, published by Chatto & Windus 1985. 'The
Washerwoman', 'Peasant Woman', 'Mother-to-be in the Milk Bar',
'She Doesn't Want To', 'Her Greatest Love', 'She Realised', 'The
Cow Loves Her', 'No Holds Barred', 'In the Railway Station', 'Her
Belly', 'Two Old Women', 'Immortal', in *No Holds Barred*, ed. the
Raving Beauties, The Women's Press, 1985. 'Two Old Women',
'Rebellion', 'Her Belly', 'Her Greatest Love', in *Spare Rib*, May
1985. 'Her Hand', 'Motherhood', 'My Daughter', in *Women's
Review*, November 1985.

Illustrations © Jola Scicińska

British Library Cataloguing in Publication Data
Swir, Anna
  Fat like the Sun
  I. title
  891.8'517   PG7178.W/

  ISBN 0-7943-4015-1

Typeset by M.C. Typeset Limited, Chatham, Kent
Reproduced, printed and bound in Great Britain by
Hazell Watson & Viney Limited,
Member of the BPCC Group,
Aylesbury, Bucks

Contents

Preface

Our second anthology of women's poetry, *No Holds Barred*, was to be exclusively British. But when we were sent a selection of Anna Swir's work, translated by Margaret Marshment and Grazyna Baran, we decided to make an exception. Her translators had found publishers reluctant, and we wanted to give Swir some exposure, however modest. That desire finally led to this book, which contains a substantial selection of her work. She can at last be established as a major poet outside her own country, Poland, where she is already respected as such.

Swir exemplified the general style of *No Holds Barred* – anti-heroic, direct and uncompromising, but also capable of great tenderness. Many of the women she writes about exist in brutal situations, yet they are described with reverence and love: at whatever level of degradation they exist, these women are precious and their worth is a powerful endictment of the terrible conditions they endure. Swir chooses a critical moment in each of their lives, and the simplicity of her description achieves an operatic intensity. She rescues each woman from her 'insignificance' in the blind eye of the world, and presents us with the tragedy of her wasted life. In isolating these tragic conditions, Swir gives her sisters, 'just the same as me underneath', their dignity as human beings.

In *Three Loves* Swir is equally powerful when she writes subjectively. This poetry moves from breathtaking images of sexual ecstasy to explosions of vehement self-disgust in a journey towards equilibrium. She is as trapped by her sex and sexuality as the other woman she has written about, but she cannot be as compassionate towards herself. Her deep attachment to the self-immolating pleasures of the body and the remorseless cycle of pleasure and pain which they breed become loathsome to her; yet she compels us with her perceptions of 'the joy of the pain of love'.

The inevitable unity of pleasure and pain also dominates the descriptions of the double face of motherhood in the extracts from *The Wind*. Anna's 'darling girl' is at once redemption and death, and motherhood is synonymous with 'the inhuman virtue of sacrifice'.

A woman like Swir, painfully aware of the duality of life, defies easy definition. She rejected labels of any kind, and the best tribute to her free spirit is written by herself:

> I will not be the slave to any love.
> To no one
> will I hand over my purpose in life,
> my right to go on growing
> to my very last breath.

Anna Carteret
Sue Jones-Davies
Fanny Viner

Foreword: Translating Anna Swir

I was introduced to Anna Swir's poetry in Poland by a colleague who lent me a volume of her work. To my dismay it was in Polish, and I didn't read Polish. But I was so eager to read the 'only feminist poet' in Poland that I got out my dictionaries and grammar books and sat down to translate one short poem. It took me a whole evening. It was a wonderful poem: 'The Cow Loves Her'. So the next evening I translated another one. That was wonderful too: 'Her Belly'. Over the next few months I translated the whole of *I'm the Old Woman* in this way. I still couldn't read Polish, but I was learning. Painstakingly looking up every word, every grammatical ending, puzzling over the resulting jigsaw of words on the page (Polish being an inflected language, word order within a sentence is not fixed), moved to tears of joy when the meaning finally leapt at me.

I had done it for myself: to be able to read Anna Swir's work. It was Grazyna, back in England, who suggested I share it with women here and offered her help in the project. Thus began our working partnership. 'I'm the Pole and she's the poet,' is how she would introduce us, but it couldn't have worked if that had really been the case; in practice our roles had to overlap, we were translating a Polish poet, we had each to learn to be both.

For *I'm the Old Woman* and *Felicity's Love* we had the help of Anna Swir herself, then still alive in Kraków. With English-speaking friends, she went through every line of our translations, questioning individual words, the order of words, the arrangements of lines, punctuation. She was so thorough we sent explanations with our drafts; she chose between offered alternatives, answered our questions, made criticisms, interpreted her own work for us and even occasionally changed it to make its meaning clearer in English. When she died in 1984 our grief was for a sister, a friend and a co-worker. We have missed her help in our later work, but we came to know her as a poet so well that we hope we can judge what she might or might not mean accurately enough to repay her trust in us as translators of her brilliant and powerful poetry.

From the start we were clear that our aim was to translate Anna Swir's poems literally into English poems: as accurate as a prose translation, as moving as the originals in their poetic effect. We never entertained the idea that this aim could be divided into conflicting criteria of accuracy and poetry. On the contrary, only by strict fidelity to the original Polish could we render Anna Swir's meaning with the same emotive impact. It would be presumptuous to claim complete success: aside from those errors and shortcomings which others will see more clearly than us, we are aware of idioms, words and phrases whose English equivalents lack connotations of the Polish, of puns that don't exist in English, of the 'feel' of a word being different outside the context of Polish experience, of the impossibility of always being able to follow her line endings and syntactical stresses. But English has its own contribution to make Anna Swir's meaning: fortuitous puns, associations or sound echoes in a literal translation that reinforce the original meaning, ways of giving stress to words through rhythm as well as syntax.

If the result is a slight anglicisation of Anna Swir's meaning, we believe this to be fully consonant with her aims as a poet. She wrote for workers and peasants and these are among her most avid readers in Poland. She also wrote for women, whose liberation she considered 'the most important cause in the world today'. There is a general absence in her work of aspects of history and culture that are specifically Polish, so that while her poetry deals with the material experience of Polish women, and to readers with know-ledge of Poland will undoubtedly appear very evocative of that country, there is much in common with women's material experi-ence everywhere, and it is this which is also Anna Swir's subject.

Her language is the concrete language of everyday speech because her subject is women's everyday lives. It is extreme because ordinary life is extreme, whether it be the simple but terrible truth that women, who 'gave birth to the world', have been 'robbed of [their lives]', or the transcendent experiences of birth and death, or the excesses of emotion involved in sexual love. These are contradictory experiences: common but extraordinary, painful but natural, transcendent but transient; and Anna Swir captures these contradictions in images that are simple, shocking, grotesque and beautiful. And they are contradictions, not ambiguities. For the most part she eschews the subtle complexities that literary establishments have so often praised as the hallmark of poetic excellence. Perhaps it is these that make poetry 'difficult', and difficult to translate. Perhaps therefore we are lucky in our task as translators to have chosen a poet like Anna Swir. But we would rather think that we chose her because she has a forceful vision of women's lives that speaks to us everywhere, across boundaries of man's making, boundaries of nation, language and mystifying literary forms.

Anna Świrszczyńska, who adopted the pen-name Anna Swir, was born in Warsaw on 7 February 1909, where she was brought up and went to university. However, she also spent much time in the Polish countryside with her artist father, and it is thought that this is where she developed her insight into Polish peasant life, which is so evident in *I'm the Old Woman*.

She lived in Warsaw throughout the war and occupation, where she worked as a waitress and participated in the literary underground. During the fighting in 1939 and again during the Warsaw uprising of 1944 she served as an orderly and nurse in hospitals. After the war she lived in Kraków, writing poetry, plays and stories, and plays for children. She published nine volumes of poetry, including one on the Warsaw uprising, and some ten plays, as well as works for radio and television. She was a feminist in a country without a women's movement, a vegetarian in a country that prides itself on its meats and sausages, and a teetotaller in a country famous for its vodka. Her hobbies were walking and yoga; she started jogging in her fifties and became interested in Indian music in her seventies. She was married, with one daughter, and later divorced. An intensely private person, she avoided the limelight for herself.

In September 1984, Anna Swir died of pneumonia after an operation.

Very little of her work has been translated into English: a limited dual-language edition of *Budowałam Barykadę* by Magnus J. Krynski and Robert A. Maguire in Kraków, and a selection in an American anthology by Czesław Miłosz. This is the first substantial volume of her work to be published in England.

Margaret Marshment

Acknowledgements

The translators would like to thank the many friends and colleagues who have helped them in translating these poems, in obtaining copies of the original Polish and in communicating with the poet and her estate. In particular we would like to thank: Anna Świrszczyńska; her daughter, Ludmila Adamska; Krystyna Stamirowska, Teresa Bela and Anna Walczuk of the Jagiellonian University, Kraków; and Maria Jastrzębska and Ania Corless, library staff at POSK in London.

Three Loves

Woman Speaks to Her Thigh

It's due entirely to your beauty
that I can take part
in the rites of love.

The mystical ecstasies,
the small betrayals exquisite
as scarlet lipstick,
the perverse rococo
convolutions of the psyche,
the sweetness of sensual longing
choking the breath in my breast,
the craters of despair
descending to the world's utmost depths –
all these I owe to you.

I ought to whip you tenderly each day
with jets of ice-cold water,
since it's you permits me to win
the loveliness and wisdom
which nothing can replace.

The souls of lovers open before me
in the moment of love
and I have them in my power.
Like a sculptor regarding
his work, I gaze
at their eyelid-locked faces,
tormented with ecstasy,
thickened
with joy.
Like an angel
I read the thoughts
inside their skulls.
I feel in the palm of my hand

the beating of their human hearts,
I hear the words
they whisper to each other
in life's sincerest moment.

I enter their souls
and wander
along the road of rapture or horror
to lands as unfathomed
as the ocean beds.
Then, loaded with treasures,
I return, slowly,
to myself.

Oh, so many riches,
so many priceless truths,
growing ever greater in metaphysical echo,
so much secret knowledge,
subtle and awesome,
do I owe to you, my thigh.

The most perfect beauty of soul
would give me no such treasures
were it not for your bright smooth charm;
you amoral little animal.

4

Felicity's Love

Three Bodies

The pregnant woman
lies at night beside her man.
The child moves
inside her belly.
– Put your hand on my belly,
says the woman.
That tiny movement you can feel
is our child's
tiny arm or leg.
The child will be mine and yours,
though I alone must bear it.

The man snuggles up to her.
They're both feeling the same thing.
The child moves inside the woman.

And the three bodies
merge their warmths
at night, when the pregnant woman
lies beside her man.

Blue Pyjamas

I sleep in blue pyjamas,
on my right sleeps my child.
I have never cried.
I will never die.

I sleep in blue pyjamas,
on my left sleeps my man.
I have never beat my head against the wall.
I have never cried out in terror.

How wide this bed is
to have room
for so much happiness.

You Are Warm

You are as warm
as a big dog. I bask
in your warmth. I'm submerged
in purity.

Every day I place around my neck
the pearls of your youthful rapture.
I plait your tenderness into my hair.
Your serenity
strokes my brow.

You have the innocent magic
of someone who has never known
the kiss of suffering or the embrace of fear.

I lean over
and look into your eyes.
Unruffled by thought, they reflect
the sky.

The Pineal Gland

You lie sleeping
as hot as a small boiler-room.
Your lungs move, your intestines digest,
your glands work zealously,
from the biochemical processes of sleep
bloom
the flora of dreams.

Do you belong to me?
My own self
doesn't belong to me.

I touch my skin,
my lungs move inside me,
my intestines digest,
my body performs its work,
about which I know so little.
I don't know the function of the pineal gland.
What really connects me
to my body?

I touch your skin
and my skin,
I am not in you
and I am not in me.
How cold.

Homeless and shivering, I look
at our two bodies,
so warm and still.

You're Already Asleep

As you drop off to sleep
you ask me if I'm happy.

Over our bed stands death
looking at me
through your body as through glass
with its bare
lidless eyes.

Under our bed
is an abyss to the stars.

Cover my eyes with your hands
my warm-blooded man.
Cover my eyes with your living hands.

You're already asleep.

Female and Male

You impregnated me and I bore pearls.
Genuine ones. Look.

You stare in amazement,
you're appalled by this wealth
which you don't understand.

You stone, who have set an avalanche in motion,
see how its breathless
splendour shines.
Hear the weighty anthem
of its fall.

You stone, with no eyes or ears.

Amazement

I'd looked at you
for so many years
that you'd become quite invisible.
But I didn't realise it.

Yesterday
I chanced to kiss someone else.
And only then
did I learn with amazement
that you'd ceased
long ago
to be a man to me.

He Went Away

I was touched by the finger of death.
The world
fell in on me.

I lie beneath the rubble,
arms smashed,
legs smashed,
back broken.

In the distance
are some people walking by.
I call out. They don't hear.
They carry on walking.
I am dying.

The man who's closest comes over.
He looks for a moment.
Can comprehend nothing.
He goes away.

He's got a good heart,
he's gone to comfort someone else.

Parting

Our love had taken years to die.
And now our parting
has suddenly revived it.
Our love has risen from the dead
as gruesome
as a corpse brought back to life
in order to die
a second time.

Every night we make love,
every hour we make up our minds to part,
every hour
we swear to be true to each other till death.

We suffer as acutely
as the damned suffer in hell.
We both have
incredibly high fevers.

Groaning with hatred
we drag out the wedding photographs.
And for whole nights, till the whiteness of dawn,
weeping, making love,
perspiring with the sweat of death,
we talk to each other,
we talk to each other,
we talk to each other
for the first and last time in our lives.

As I Need Air

I shall defile my body,
which you have loved.
I need to, to live, as I need air.
I shall defile you
in defiling my body.

It's impossible to love someone defiled.
I shall be saved.

A Razor

I have betrayed you.
What happiness, what relief.
Let's both rejoice
that now
I can love you like before.

Let's both rejoice
that I had to betray you,
like a drowning person
has to grab at a razor.

I hate you
because I've betrayed you.
Let's both rejoice
that I hate you.

Tears Flow

They are dying, naked, nestled together,
bound together by suffering
as once by love.
Incapable of living together,
indispensable to each other in this moment of death,
nearest to each other
in just this moment.

Their embrace is of ice,
they are departing together, fulfilling the oath
of till death us do part.

Her tears
stream on to his naked shoulder,
his tears flow
between her naked breasts.

Then
they both freeze
like sculptures on an Etruscan coffin.

Clean

How many casual lovers
will it take to kill the memory in me?

How good it is to defile oneself,
now it's spring, I'll defile myself
in a spring forest.
I'll give my lovers my laughter.

As I become cleaner and cleaner
the more I remember
how clean you were.

You Died

You really died in me, not when
another gave me joy.
You died in me
when another gave me pain.

You Died

You really died in me, not when
another gave me joy.
You died in me
when another gave me pain.

To Re-create Myself

What I want
is to get away from my hand,
from the two eyes that look at me in the mirror,
from my right leg,
my left leg,
and all the rest of me.

I have an absolute need
to exist somewhere else.
An ecstatic need to exist
as someone else.
What I want
is to re-create myself.

It's not essential for me to live,
but is it essential that
I re-create myself.

Open the Door of Sleep

Come to me
in my sleep.
You are dead,
I am dead.
Come for a last night of love
of two beings who no longer exist.

It doesn't matter that I hate you,
it doesn't matter that you hate me.
That someone else is with me now.
Deceive the vigilance
of your thoughts, which are my enemies.
Deceive the vigilance
of my heart, which no longer loves you.
Gently,
open the door of sleep.
Come to me.

In my sleep
that which has happened hasn't happened yet.
So you will kiss me
with the lips of our young love,
and I will speak to you more tenderly
than I ever spoke in life.

It doesn't matter that you hate me,
it doesn't matter that I hate you.
You are dead,
I am dead,
come to me.

My Fireproof Smile

I've discovered a strength in myself,
and no one can take it from me.
No man
is irreplaceable.
I've paid the price
for this knowledge.

I've passed through a bath of fire,
and how perfectly
fire fortifies.
I've salvaged from it
my fireproof smile.
I'll never again ask anyone
to lay their hand on my brow.
I'll rely
on myself.

I'm as closed as a medieval city
with its drawbridge raised.
You may kill this city,
but no one will get in.

My Body is Froth

I have been born again.
I am as light
as the eyelash of the wind.
I am foaming. I am foam.

I go dancing alone,
if I want to, I can rise into the air.
The concentrated lightness
of my body
is particularly concentrated
in the lightness
of my feet and my ten toes.

My feet skim over the earth,
which bends like compressed air.
A buoyant duet
of earth and feet. A dance
of liberation.

I have been born again,
the world's happiness
is mine once more.
My body is froth,
one thinks with one's body,
and mine is froth.

If I want to,
I can rise into the air.

Antonia's Love

Orphans

When you come to me at night
you're an animal.
Only night
can marry a woman and an animal.
You could be a wild goat
or a mad dog.
One can't see in the dark.

I murmur sweet nothings.
You don't understand, you're an animal.
You never wonder
why I cry.

But your animal body
understands better than you.
It too is sad.
And when you fall asleep
its hairy warmth comforts me.
We sleep snuggled up together
like two orphaned puppies.

A Sad Conversation at Night

– You ought to have lots of lovers.
– Yes, love.
– I've had plenty of women.
– I've had men, love.
– I'm no good.
– I know, love.
– Don't trust me.
– I don't, love.
– I'm afraid of dying.
– So am I, love.
– You won't leave me.
– No, love.
– I'm alone.
– Me too, love.
– Cuddle up to me.
– Goodnight, love.

A Wild Cat's Tongue

Our love is as rough
as a wild cat's tongue.

We love each other
in a hammock of fire,
in the sunny entrails
of the sun.

We love each other
like two birds of prey
in the lightning flash
of their mating.

We love each other
in silence.

The Door is Open

No, I don't want to tame you,
you'd lose your animal charm.
Your wiliness and nervousness
excite me,
they belong to your exotic breed.

You can't escape
because the door is always open.
You can't betray me
because I don't demand fidelity.

Give me your hand,
we'll dance
through the laughing darkness.
With sacred bells
on our arms and legs,
the movement of the dance
as supple as ancient Arabic writing,
our hair singing
like a Greek chorus.

Elemental bliss
organised into a mystery play.
Only just domesticated,
like you.

Love Divides the Lovers

You're jealous
of the joy you give me,
because I betray you
with it.
What you give me as a trickle
explodes in me
as a river.

It lifts me up
far beyond your reach,
to paradises
you will never know
and never understand.

We are foreigners, enemies,
singing our love songs
in different languages.
Your body's no more than an instrument
for giving joy
to my body,
which is much the more
chivalrous arrangement.

I won't be submerged in you.
I want you to be submerged
in me.

My laughing egoism
defends and adorns my nakedness,
it's a lifebelt.

The skin divides two beating hearts,
the love divides the lovers.
The beautiful song of the night
is a song of war.

A Spring

The greatest joy you give me
is the joy of not loving you.
Freedom.

When I'm with you I bask
in that freedom.
I can be gentle
because I am strong.
Tender
because I am tensed like a spring.

In my every embrace
is a readiness to leave.
Like a leap
held ready in an athlete's body.

I Cannot

I envy you.
At any moment
you can leave me.

But I cannot
leave myself.

An Iron Comb

Don't come round today.
If I did answer the door
you wouldn't recognise me.
Because today I'm stocktaking,
doing general repairs,
an annual balance sheet,
spring cleaning.
A dress rehearsal for the end of the world
in microcosm.

With an iron comb
I'm scrubbing my body down to the bone.
I've taken my skin off and hung it up on a nail,
my exposed innards are steaming,
my exposed ribs are shaking,
while the court –
the highest of high courts,
from which there is no appeal –
proceeds to pass judgement.
All its verdicts
are 'guilty'.

It passes judgement on my brain and my eyes,
which I've removed from my skull,
on the wicked nakedness of my pelvis,
on my teeth, which I've removed from their gums,
on my dirty lungs, on my lazy shinbones.

Oh, I'm taking great pains today,
with an iron comb
I'm scrubbing my body down to the bone,
the bone down to the marrow.
I want to be cleaner than a bone.
I want to be as clean as nothingness.

I am the jury, I am the judge,
I'm shaking with terror,
I am the condemned and the overworked executioner.
I'm drawing up a balance sheet,
I'm sweating blood.

So don't come round today.
Don't buy me flowers.
It'd be a waste of money.

Go to the Cinema

I'm equally happy
whether you're arriving or leaving.
So you give me
two kinds of happiness.

But don't come round today.
I have guests. They're called
Bored with Romantic Ritual,
Eternity's Sneer, and
Disgust.

They're foreigners. You don't know their language.
Better go to the cinema
and see a western.

Just the Same Underneath

On my way to your place
I noticed an old beggar woman
on a street corner.

I took hold of her hand
and kissed her on her delicate cheek,
we chatted for a while, she was
just the same as me underneath,
the same sort of person,
I sensed it at once,
the way a dog senses the smell
of another dog.

I gave her some money,
I couldn't leave her.
After all, everyone needs
someone close to them.

And then I wondered what
I was coming to your place for.

The Large Intestine

Look in the mirror, let's both look.
That's my naked body.
You seem to like it,
but I've no cause to.
Who bound us together, me and my body?
Why do I have to die
when it dies?
I've a right to know where the dividing line
between us is.
Where I am, I myself, my self.

My stomach, am I in my stomach? In my intestines?
In my vagina? In my toe?
In my brain, it seems. But I can't see my brain.
Take it out of my skull. I've a right
to look at myself. Don't laugh.
I'm being gruesome, you say.

It wasn't me
who made my body.
I inherited scraps from my family:
an alien brain – the product of chance, hair
from my grandmother, a nose
cobbled together from several dead noses.
What connects me
to all this?
What connects me
to you who like
my knee? What on earth have I
in common with my knee?
If it'd been up to me
I'd have chosen a quite different model.

I'll go off and leave you together,
you and my knee.
Don't pull a face, I'll leave you my whole body

to play with.
And I'll go.
There's no place for me here
in this blind carnality, just waiting
to rot.
I'll run away, I'll run as fast as I can
towards my self.
I'll go and search for my self,
running
like a madwoman
till I drop.

I'll have to hurry, before death
arrives. Because then,
straining like a dog on a chain,
I'll have to return
to my noisily suffering body.
To perform its last
and noisiest rites.

Defeated by my body,
obliterated because of my body,
I amount to no more
than a failed kidney
or a gangrenous large intestine.
And I die in ignominy.

But with me dies the universe,
reduced
to a failed kidney
or a gangrenous large intestine.

You Can't Reach

So much shame
in our women's despair.
So much carolling of birds
in our debauchery.

Your suffering
is as brazen as your body.
You cry
as shamelessly as a baby.
I despise you then.

You men are so obvious and ponderous,
how can you possibly understand
those whose bodies are as light
as a peal of laughter.
You know nothing
of the irrepressible courage of a flame
that constantly consumes itself
to be constantly transformed.
We have that courage
in buoyant abundance.

I'm not the same person
with you
as I was with others.
From the tip of my nose down to my heels,
I'm different.
And still another person
is waiting inside me.

But when you leave
you'll take with you
a badly scratched record
with just the one tune on it.
For me, love's heaven
and love's hell
blossom so high up. You can't reach
them, even to ruin them.

In the Railway Station

There are mad old women
who carry all their property
in a little bundle on their backs.

Vagrants who curl up
at night in the railway station.
Sick people waiting in hospital
for what will be
their last operation.

And I have wasted all this time
on you.

I'll Open the Window

We made love for too long.
We loved each other
down to the bone.
I can hear the bones grinding, can see
our two skeletons.

Now I'm waiting
for you to leave, for
the clatter of your shoes
to die out on the stairs.

Quiet at last.

Tonight I'll sleep alone
between pure clean sheets.
Solitude
is the first rule of hygiene.
Solitude makes the room bigger.
I'll open the window
and let in the expansive frosty air,
as healthy as a tragedy.
I'll let in human thoughts
and human affairs,
others' griefs and others' holiness.
They'll speak quietly and sternly.

Don't come here again.
It's not often
I'm an animal.

Dance of Murder

I'm leaving.

You didn't make me suffer
so you needn't expect
my hatred.
That would be too splendid and important a gift.
You're not worth anything
as precious
as a shred of living flesh.

I've killed
your presence within me,
easily.

I'm cleansed.
I'm dancing a festive dance of murder.

Non-existent

Where are you, lover,
as pure as a plant,
more faithful
than my own body?
The earth gives birth to millions of people,
but not to you.

There isn't even
a silence waiting for your voice,
not even a space
waiting for the shadow of the movement
of your arm.

Non-existent,
come to me.

No Holds Barred

I catch hold of different things:
snow, trees, useless telephone calls,
the tenderness of a child, journeys,
Rózewicz's poetry,
sleep, apples, morning exercises,
conversations about the salutary properties of vitamins,
exhibitions of avant-garde art,
walks on Kościuszko's mound, politics,
Penderecki's music,
natural disasters in foreign countries,
the joy of morality and the joy of immorality,
gossip, a cold shower, fashion magazines from abroad,
learning Italian,
a fondness for dogs, the calendar.

I catch hold of everything,
so as not to fall
into the abyss.

Stephanie's Love

A Kind World

Fra Angelico's heaven
unites us.
His childlike angels
beckon us.

We'll carry his smile in our rucksacks
as we roam together
through a springlike world
as kind as the death of the blessed.

Fetters

Like tying my hair with silk ribbons
I've adorned myself in submission.
Silk is strong.
It makes good fetters.

In a Meadow

One white daisy
and my two closed eyes.
These shield us from the world.

Two Fledgling Angels

When you kissed me for the first time
we turned into
two fledgling angels
whose wings were just about
to bud.

Stilled in mid-gesture,
hushed in mid-breath,
awed
to the marrow,
their bodies listen
as the first tiny feathers
sprout from their shoulders.

Sleepy Eyelashes

I yearn for the meadow
where our warm kisses
were left in a hollow
of crushed grass.

I yearn for the forest
where the sleepy eyelashes
of our two sighs embracing
got entangled
in the springtime moss.

In a Purple Gondola

It's not you I love, but the happiness
I give you.

It's what unites us.
The way a purple gondola unites
a young doge and his bride
on their wedding day.

Our Innards Shimmer

You've given me bliss.
I've given you bliss.
Immaculate,
we gaze into each other's
eyes.

In each of our bodies
sexuality shines
as pure as amber.
Under our skins
our innards shimmer.

You've given me purity.
I've given you purity.
The most perfect purity
in the world.

The Song of the Happy Woman

A song of excess,
strength, potent sensitivity,
supple ecstasy.
Splendour
dancing tenderly.

I tremble like a body in bliss,
I tremble like a wing,
I am an explosion,
I transcend myself,
I am a fountain
with a fountain's buoyancy.
Excess,
a thousand excesses,
strength,
a song of gushing strength.

In me are gifts
of effloresence and profusion,
ringlets of light sobbing,
fire foaming, with its ethereal
ripeness ripening.
Oceans of radiance leap up convulsively
as pink as a mouth
wide open in ecstasy.

I'm up to my eyes
in amazement, I snort.
A snorting universe
of amazement engulfs me.
I gulp down excess,
I choke on a plenitude
as impossible
as reality.

First Madrigal

That night of love
was as pure
as an ancient musical instrument
and the air
around it.

It was as sumptuous
as a coronation feast.
As carnal
as a pregnant belly.
As abstract
as a number.

It was only a moment of life,
yet it wanted to be the culmination of life.
A transient moment,
and it wanted to master the meaning of the world.

That night of love
had ambitions.

Second Madrigal

A night of love
as elegant
as an old Venetian concert
played on elegant old instruments.
As wholesome
as a baby angel's bottom.
As wise
as an anthill.
As vivid
as a trumpet blast.
As sumptuous
as the court
of a pair of barbarian monarchs
seated on two golden thrones.

A night of love with you,
a mighty baroque battle
with two victors.

An Iron Hedgehog

As happy
as a foetus in the womb
I sleep hidden inside you.

Don't let me be born yet.
I want to stay inside you for ever.
In here I am warm
and safe.

Right now I don't exist outside you,
I've no existence anywhere else,
and it suits me fine.

The world is so frosty I fear it.
It's like a hedgehog with prickles made of iron and ice.
Don't ever let me be born.
I just want to sleep inside you.

From the Ocean Bed

I'm precious beyond price
when you are with me.
I wallow in the bath of your rapturous admiration.
Your rapture
has created me.

I am the fountainhead from which you drink
happiness.
To be a fountainhead of happiness –
it's so magnificent.

You sing me,
my body is born of your song.
It's immortal, and perfectly beautiful,
because it doesn't really exist.

I make you happy,
so I can make you suffer.
You presented me with this power.
I'm blossoming. You've made me a queen.
My blossoming enraptures you,
we're both in bliss
because of my blossoming.

I can make you suffer. You're afraid.
Defenceless. I can feel your fear.
Your fear arouses my cruelty.
I look at it amazed
as if it were a beast from the ocean bed.

We're both amazed
at its lightning agility.
Your fear entices it.
They lead each other on
like young cats at play,
each getting more and more beautiful

as they entice each other.
Until they're both incredibly beautiful:
my cruelty
and your defencelessness.

This is a fascinating game, my love.
Let's put a stop to it.

I Sweat and Puff

You cultivate me
as you would your own insanity,
or a rare cactus.
Lost in admiration,
you do it
with commendable zeal.

You're training me.
You kneel before me.
That's how you train
a saint.

I have to be a seraphim too,
with six wings,
and give you mystical joy
the way cows give milk.

I try as hard as I can.
I sweat and puff,
my eyes pop out of my head
with the effort.

I trot along obediently
in the dog-collar of your adoration.

Disappointed and Happy

I see a man walking in front of me.
Slim hips, as slender
as smoke from a chimney.

He's carrying inside him
his own masculine mind, unknown to me,
the mystery – one might say –
of masculinity.

He turns round.
It's only my own man, after all.
I didn't recognise him in a different coat.
His glamour vanishes,
this citadel is already captured.

I hold out my hand and smile.
Disappointed and happy
I run towards him
as if towards myself.

Like a Baby

Your love is killing mine.
You love me
too passionately.

Why should I make any effort?
You weep enough for us both
with your desire and your jealousy.

Your love grows more and more beautiful,
you're the mystical bush in Dante's paradise,
a fountain of ecstatic flames
that towers above me
more bravely every day.

You flourish
in your suffering. While I'm withering away
like a limb
that isn't used.

I've already forgotten what it means to suffer.
I'll soon have the spiritual life
of a baby.

A Genius

I'm bored with my body.
For years I've tried
to train it.
I've starved it, poured icy water on it,
whipped it assiduously
with irony.
To no purpose.

It's dull,
it has no ambition.
It'll never be a genius,
like a yogi's body.

One of these nights
I'll leave it in your arms
and go away.

I need a break.

When We Wake Up

I'm so glad it happened,
and I'm so glad it's over now.
I've you to thank, my love,
for both these joys.

Now
my body is light
and my soul is clean.
I've been dry-cleaned of my lust,
and now I passionately desire
some hard labour,
some heavy human work.

Work is what my head wants,
work is what my hands want.
I was made for work.
Not for pleasure.
I am strong. I can carry
the heavy loads that the strong carry.

Black Poppy Seeds

We are sad.
Dread has sat down beside us.
Grief blows black
poppy seeds into our hearts.
I weep,
you put your arms around me
to console me.
From this embrace comes a sweetness,
from this sweetness a flame.

We gaze into each other's eyes,
shining with happiness.
Our bodies have consoled us.

I'm Panting

Why talk
when you can shout.
Why walk
when you can run.
Why just live
when you can blaze like fire.

I'm running and shouting with joy,
I'm running and shouting with grief.
I'm panting,
my lungs are working like mad.

Violent feelings
are supposed to be good for you.

Don't Cry

Don't cry, I'll kiss away your tears.
Your suffering
glues me to you
more firmly than your happiness.

I'll never leave you as long as
you suffer.

Kill Me

Don't kiss me, darling.
Don't embrace me, darling.
If you love me,
kill me, darling.

I Prostrate Myself

I prostrate myself
and kiss the black earth.
I say: dear God, who doesn't exist,
don't ever let me harm
a living person.

Rather than that
let my hands drop off,
let me be struck
by lightning.

I prostrate myself
and kiss the living earth.
I say: dear God, who doesn't exist
on the furthermost star,
who exists within me,
who is as perfect as I am utterly worthless,
who is a cruel God,
I'm making you a blood offering,
I'm giving back to you
the greatest happiness
of my life.

I Must Do It

My dearest love, I must leave you.
I must go away
and be alone again.
I'll have to take my body with me,
disentangle it
from the dreamlike happiness
of its embrace with your body.

It won't be easy. They've become
completely entwined
and like two cornered animals
will defend themselves
against being torn apart.
In their terror, they will put up
a senseless and beautiful
fight for their lives,
for their own law
of the night.

I must renounce you, my love –
though I know you need me –
and go away somewhere
where no one needs me.
I must shoot you through the heart –
though you beg for mercy.
I must shoot myself through the heart –
though I am afraid.

Absolutely no one
demands this of me.
Yet I must do it.

Headfirst

I kiss you and I cry.
You kiss my tears and you kiss my lips.
You're in love with my lips
and with my tears.

Clasped together, motionless,
we listen as they drop,
one by one,
into our one united heart.

I'm sinking
into the heartbreaking happiness
of love's despair.
I'm being carried away by a waterfall
of ecstasy and pain.
I'm plunging headfirst
in foaming water, foaming hair,
leaves, crashing waves.
I'm falling –
I'll be dashed to pieces on a rock,
smashed to smithereens at the bottom,
where? where? when?

I measure the magnitude of the world
by the extent of my fall.
How splendid the world must be
if one can suffer like this.
I measure the happiness of the world
by my unhappiness.
How beautiful happiness must be
if unhappiness
is so very lovely.
Only by falling
from the summit to the abyss
can one know
the summit and the abyss.

I shall possess
this breathtaking knowledge.

You kiss my tears
and you kiss my lips.
You're shaking all over, we both are,
impaled
on the joy of the pain of love.

We Are Going to Shoot It

We are going to kill our love.

It will be like
strangling a child.
It will be like
kicking a faithful dog.
It will be like
plucking the feathers
out of a living bird.

We are going to shoot it through the heart,
and it will be like
shooting oneself
through the heart.

The Padlock

Our bodies
don't want to be parted.
They've locked arms
and stare at us
in horror
like two children staring at a murderer
bearing down on them.

They're completely bewildered. Frantic,
wet with tears,
heaving with sobs,
gasping, they ask –
why.
And without waiting for an answer
they ask again,
gasping and gasping,
groaning, and pleading
for mercy.

But we
cannot take pity on them.
We will unfasten the padlock on their arms,
tear apart their entangled hairs,
and fling
the two rotten
impotent shreds
to either side of the room.

They Fuse Together

We must keep an eye on our bodies.
They've been torn apart,
but they fuse together again in their sleep.
We must watch
what they're up to when they're asleep,
so their dreams
can be plucked out
like the eyes of a medieval convict.

Maybe we should kill our bodies?
In self-defence
one's allowed to kill one's enemies.

A Plate Made of Pain

This morning
was created for me,
especially for me. Such luxury –
a vast new world.
A world of pain.

Through the window
is a genuine street
in a genuine town
belonging to this world of pain.
In here is a table, a plate, a spoon.
A spoon solid with pain, a real plate
made of pain. I'll eat
breakfast off it today.

In front of the house stands
a brand-new car with a driver.
It looks real enough, but it isn't.
It wasn't there yesterday,
it was made this morning,
especially for me. Such luxury.

No effort spared. Even the fly
sitting on the paper where I write
is a new fly,
a fly belonging to the world of pain.

I wasn't at all prepared
for this world.
This gift as exquisite and bizarre
as a diamond noose.

It amazes me. My hands
go cold in amazement.
My bulging eyelids
close silently
over my eyes.

Maidenhood

I'll have to be brave to get through
the day. All that's left
is the joy of a hopeless longing.
It's very precious.

This longing
cleanses like flying,
fortifies like effort,
and moulds the soul
the way work
moulds the body.

It's like a gymnast, or a runner
who'll never stop running. And it's what
gives him his endurance.

It nourishes
those who are strong.
It's like a window
in a high tower where a wind
of strength blows through.

This longing
is the maidenhood of happiness.

This Hopeless Longing

I feel this hopeless longing
in my innards, in my throat,
in my every hair.
My skin
is made of it.

But it's the light inside my head
that feels it most.
Even in my sleep
it doesn't die,
when my hair, my innards and my skin
all die.

Woman Speaks of Her Life

The wind drives me along the roads,
the wind, the god of change,
with its puffed-out cheeks.
I love this wind.
I'm happy
with change.

I travel through the world
in a couple
or on my own.
Equally happy
with desire or with the death of desire,
which is called fulfilment.

I'm too full of something or other.
I overflow my banks
like yeast. Yeast has
its own special kind of happiness.

I go on, never stopping,
at times joined by a man.
Then we go along together.
He says it will be for ever,
then gets lost in the dusk
like some inconsequential thing.

I go on alone,
then round the next corner
another man turns up.

I go on, never stopping.
The wind drives me along the roads.
On the roads I travel
there's always a wind blowing.

Mother
and Daughter

Her Hand

When my mother was dying
I held her hand.
When she died I burnt everything
her hand had touched.
Only my own hands
I couldn't burn.

A Dream of My Dead Mother

Last night
I held my mother close to me.
We were dancing
on the soft turf.

My body dissolved
like mist
in the soft sunlight of her love.

Our two bodies, two mists,
mingled in bliss
like before I was born.

She and I

When I was born
my mother's blood flowed
from between her legs.
We both suffered –
she more than I.

When she died
my mother's lifeblood flowed out
from between her legs.
And again we both suffered –
and again, she more than I.

The Birth of a Human Being

Just Outside Hell

From between my legs
blood drips on to the floor,
as I lumber along
hoisting in front of me my enormous belly.

Blood drips on to the hospital floor
outside the labour ward
which I'm about to enter
quaking
as if at death's door.

Hell

For twenty hours now
I've been groaning in the labour ward,
for twenty hours
the damned have been howling around me.
A moment,
and I'll start to howl.

Through the window, dawn
in the hospital garden.
I slip down off the bed
and crawl on all fours to the door.
I want to escape from hell.
I want to bear my child in the garden at dawn
on the quiet turf, in the cool of the dew.

They grab me
and put me back on the white oilcloth rack
in the torture chamber.

Just Before the Caesarean

Naked on the bare
table,
trapped in a downpour of light,
surrounded by men in white coats
and white masks,
my eyes track every movement
of the rubber-gloved hand
that's about to drive
the needle
into my spine.

The Caesarean

They tell me to keep talking
as the surgeon cuts me open with his scalpel,
they tell me to keep talking
as he yanks the child
out of the living cave of my innards.
I talk incessantly
to the young woman doctor
holding the oxygen mask
to my mouth.

Motherhood

I have borne a life.
It came screaming from my insides
and, like an Aztec deity,
demands the sacrifice of my life.
I bend over the small doll
and we look into
each other's eyes.

You won't get the better of me, I say,
I won't be the shell
of the egg you crack open
as you burst into the world,
nor the footbridge you cross to get to your own life.
I'll defend myself.

I bend over the small doll
and notice
a tiny movement in a tiny finger
which no time ago was inside me,
under whose delicate skin flows
my own blood.
And that's it – I'm submerged
by a towering bright wave
of humility.
Helpless, I drown.

Is it myself I worship
in the fruit of my own body?
Am I sacrificing myself
to the cannibal god of instinct?
Where will I summon the strength to resist
her, weak as she is?

The small doll needs me as much as she needs air.
I submit willingly to being swallowed by love,
I submit to being swallowed like air
by her tiny greedy lungs of life.

I Am a Mother Cat

My child sleeps beside me –
such happiness.
My child sighs the joys of sleep,
as warm as a small animal,
as happy as a small animal.

She embraces me in her sleep
I am a mother cat,
and she is a little kitten.
I am a mother dog
and she is a little puppy.

In the warm burrow of our bed
our night happiness purrs and sighs.

A Hair on the Pillow

Beside me sleeps my child.
I snuggle up to her.
She will save me,
she who is weaker than a blond hair
left curling on a warm pillow.

The Right to Kill

The dear little baby fly,
barely an hour old,
sits on my child's hand
and warms itself in the sun.

I've killed it.

People say flies carry germs.
Perhaps flies
say the same about people.

People are stronger.

My Daughter

I've built a house,
I've chosen a man,
I'm doing my work.
Then I'll retire and my daughter will take over.

She'll build a house,
she'll choose a man,
she'll carry on the work.

Then she'll retire.
In giving her life, I sentenced her.

Stop Dancing

My darling girl,
whose birth caused me such pain,
stop dancing for a moment.

Throw your warm arms around my neck.
Save me
from pain.

Patriarchy

I gave, my child flesh, and blood,
the pain of procreation,
and the unwearying care of a brooding hen
which withers a woman's sex and brain.

I gave days and nights by the thousand
which not even a miracle
could restore to me.
In her eyes I put wonder,
in her heart I put feeling,
in her head I put thoughts
which not even I can think through to the end.

But my child bears
the surname
of a man.

Courage

I will not be the slave to any love.
To no one
will I hand over my purpose in life,
my right to go on growing
to my very last breath.

Fettered by the dark instinct of motherhood,
gasping for love like an asthmatic for air,
it's such an effort to build in myself
my beautiful human egoism,
reserved for centuries
for men.

Against me
are all the civilisations of the world,
all the holy books of mankind,
written in a flash of lightning
by the eloquent pens of mystic angels.
Ten Mohammeds
in ten stylishly mouldy languages
threaten me with damnation
on earth and in eternal heaven.

Against me
is my own heart.
Trained for millennia
in the inhuman virtue of sacrifice.

I'm the Old Woman

Sisters in the Gutter

I have friends in the park,
old beggarwomen, madwomen.
In their eyes are rings
from which the jewels have fallen out.
We tell each other the stories of our lives
down below, in the gutter of humanity.
Sisters in the gutter,
we are fluent in the language of suffering.
We touch hands,
it helps us.

As I leave I kiss them on the cheek,
as delicate as water.

Rebellion

She ran away from the old people's home.

She sleeps in railway stations,
she tramps the streets, the fields,
shouting, singing, cursing
obscenely.

At the back of her head, behind the orbs of her eyes,
she carries – in the bone reliquary of her skull –
rebellion.

Peasant Woman

She carries on her shoulders
the house, the garden, the farm,
the cows, the pigs, the calves, and the children.

Her back wonders
why it doesn't break.
Her hands wonder
why they don't fall off.
She doesn't wonder.

Like a bloodstained stick
her dead mother's drudgery
sustains her.
They used the lash
on her great-grandmother.

That lash
shines on her through the clouds
instead of the sun.

Waking Up

The century of sleep
which her mother and great-grandmother
never got enough of
lies heavy on her head
when the alarm clock crows
like a rooster in the morning
at three a.m.

Made of Lead

At nightfall
she lugs herself to bed,
where her old man is snoring.

On the edge of the bed
she deposits her body.
Made of lead.

Biography of a Countrywoman

Panting
she heaves pails against her belly.

Panting
she heaves sacks on her back.

Panting
she drags buckets from the well.

Panting
she bears the fruits of man's lust.

Panting
she dies.

He Treats Them to Ice-cream

Every Sunday they went for a walk together.
He, she
and the three children.

One night
when she tried to stop him going
to his other woman,
he pulled out a flick-knife
from under the mattress.

They still go for a walk
every Sunday,
he, she and the three children.
He treats them to ice-cream and they all laugh.
She too.

Lucky Woman

There was the stylish white dress,
the registry office,
the cascading veil and the organ
in church.

There was the costly reception,
where the vodka flowed.

There was the pain
of the wedding night.

There was the handsome young husband.
But there wasn't a single
word of love.

The Children Will Be Surprised

Silently
the door closed when he left.
The sleeping children
didn't stir.

Only at daybreak will they be surprised
at their home
collapsing in the night
so silently.

He Promised

He punched her in the face
at a party.

She fell,
the people grabbed him by the arms,
he was reeling.

Later they returned together,
arms around each other.
She was smiling happily.
She was pregnant, and he'd promised
to marry her.

Branded

They smeared her door
with human faeces.

They went quiet
when she entered the shop.

They whistled at her from behind the fence
as one whistles
at a dog.

They spat at her feet
when she went to church.

When the author of her misery
passed her in the street
he turned his head
the other way.

Stepfather and Stepdaughter

With every look
and every look averted,
with every word
and every word unspoken,
he reminds her,
every day of the week, of the month, of the year,
that she's illegitimate.

The Washerwoman

She washes her old man's dirty clothes,
her sons' dirty clothes,
her daughters' dirty clothes.

Inhumanly clean
like her murdered life,
she wipes away at times the sinful tear of a dream
with her clean
washerwoman's hands.

God's Gift to Women

She went to the pub to look for him.
He came swaggering out,
hands in his pockets,
a young buck, God's gift to women,
better-looking than before he was married.

He glanced with a laugh
at her belly,
swollen with its fourth pregnancy.

She Washed the Floor

He came back after midnight,
and collapsed in the doorway.
She heaved him
into the house.

He tumbled into bed
with his boots on, vomiting,
he made a grab for her, she wouldn't have it,
he punched her in the stomach,
and started to snore.

She washed the floor,
changed the cover on the eiderdown,
and knocked on her neighbours' door.

She's about to give birth.

The Husband's Homecoming

Step by step
she retreats.

The table won't protect her,
the child's cot won't protect her,
the wall won't conceal her.

The people on the other side
of the wall won't defend her
against the man standing
in the doorway.

Pay-day

She puts her hands
in his jacket pocket
when he's asleep.

She counts the money.
She cries.

Family Life

He goes for her
with his fists.

He flicks off
like a fly from his breeches
the two small hands
that try to stop him.

A Girl of Six

He collapsed into the mud,
his snores filling the street.

Next to him
huddled up crying
is a girl of six.

Glances

As they passed
the young lads glanced
at the old woman.

And in that split second
their glances
had crushed her underfoot like a worm.

The Cow Loves Her

Her children
have long since ceased to write to her.
Now
only the cow loves her.

It's only natural,
after all she's cared for it
since it was born.

Mother and Son

The young fist
is raised above the grey head.

The young fist
smashes open the door with a bang.

The grey head
drops into her hands.

She Doesn't Remember

She was a bad stepmother.
In her old age she's dying
in a deserted shack.

She's shivering
like a handful of burnt paper.
She doesn't remember now that she was bad.
But she knows
that she's cold.

Two Old Women

The two of us sit in the doorway,
chatting about our children and grandchildren.
We sink happily
into our oldwomanhood.

Like two spoons
sinking
into a bowl of hot porridge.

Her Belly

She has a right to have a fat belly,
her belly has borne five children.
They warmed themselves at it,
it was the sun of their childhood.

The five children have gone,
her fat belly remains.
This belly
is beautiful.

The Reaper

Fat like the sun,
panting in the sun,
she hurls into the panting threshing-machine
the panting suns
of sheaves.

Immortal

She moved out of herself
a long time ago.

With each new grandchild
she begins life anew
like a river constantly renewed
from its source.

Gazing always at the sky
with the eyes of the newborn
she won't notice
the death of her body.

Her Greatest Love

At sixty she's experiencing
the greatest love of her life.

She walks arm in arm with her lover,
the wind ruffles their grey hairs.

Her lover says:
– You have hair like pearls.

Her children say:
– You silly old fool.

Mother-to-be in the Milk Bar

The very young mother-to-be
pours milk into a mug.
After eight hours on her feet
her legs are puffy.

But in her heart there flies about
on little rose-coloured wings
the little bib
she bought the day before.

She Can't Sleep

At night the girl
sits curled up on the bed.
She looks at the boy
who sleeps beside her.

At night the girl
sits curled up on the bed.
She looks at the window.
Not long till dawn.

The Ambulance

Her lips are trembling,
as she is carried to the ambulance
she can hear
her husband's snoring.

Death

We give birth to life
in the company of death.
Silent
she stands under the clock
in the delivery room.

She listens to the screams,
she counts
the ebbs and flows of pain,
she follows
the midwife's fingers unscrewing the tap
on the oxygen cylinder.

As alert as an actor
awaiting
his cue.

The Ward Orderly

Day and night
she carries people's
urine, blood and faeces.

A fat woman
always laughing and telling
dirty jokes.

That's her way of coping
with the people's urine, blood and faeces
that she carries
day and night.

A Normal Delivery

For twenty hours
she yells like an animal.
The doctor wants to help her.
He cuts her living flesh with scissors –
without anaesthetic.

She didn't feel it.
Too intense
is the torture tearing her bones apart.

What Satan
invented the world?

The Midwife

Walking amid the flames of hell,
listening to the howls of the damned,
she feels at home
in hell.

Inflicting pain,
stroking the sweat-matted hair.
Saying little. Shouting.

Her awesomely clean hands
are wise and sad
like God.

Like Carrion

Stripped of her skin,
defiled like a woman being raped,
like a woman
they're through with raping,
like a corpse slapped in the face,
like someone spat at
on their death bed,
like a living animal
dying in the slaughterhouse
to be made into food products,
degraded like carrion,
despising herself,
like carrion's excrement,
humiliated
more profoundly
than a man
can ever be humiliated –

a woman
on the gynaecologist's table
under the gaze
of the doctors.

The Taming of the Shrew

A renaissance actor
brandishing a whip
chases across the stage a girl
who rebelled
against the fate
of girls.

Men of the twentieth century
applaud.

Old Woman

Her beauty
is like Atlantis.
It has yet to be discovered.

A thousand humorists have written
about her sexual hunger.
The most brilliant of them
have found their way into the schoolbooks.
Only her affair with the Devil
has been graced with the gravity
of the pyre.
And like a pyre
has lived in man's imagination.

Mankind has invented for her
the most abusive
language in the world.

She Doesn't Want To

Her mother
suffered her whole life.
And bore her
to suffer too.

But she doesn't want to suffer.
She hates
her mother.

She stretches her fists to the sky,
and with her fists
she writes across the sky
from horizon to horizon:
– I don't want to.

A Dark Star

Born under a dark star
we gave birth
to the world.